LIVING IN THE REALM OF REVELATION

By

Phillip Rich

Ekklisia Prophetic
APOSTOLIC MINISTRIES, INC.

Published By Ekklisia Ministries

Copyright 2006 A. D.

All rights reserved under International Copyright law. No part of this publication may be reproduced, stored in a retrieval system, or transmitted, in whole or in part, in any form or by any means, electronic, mechanical, photocopying, recording or otherwise, without the prior express consent of the publisher. All scripture is the Kings James Version unless otherwise stated. All rights reserved.

Take note that the name satan is not capitalized. We choose not to acknowledge him, even to the point of violating grammatical rules

Table of Contents

How to Live in the Realm of Revelation 1

How to Increase the Power of Revelation In Your Life . 10

Revelation Gifts 25

Revelation Secrets 37

Impartation Increases Revelation 58

Chapter 1

How to Live in the Realm of Revelation

Without revelation, there is no manifestation. Everything we get from God comes by the revelation of the Holy Spirit. You can't prosper, be healed, saved, delivered, walk in victory or have a relationship with God outside of a revelation by the Holy Spirit.

When I minister to people and the Holy Spirit reveals names, illnesses and other things to me. We are seeing the gifts of the Holy Spirit in action. I have had people come up to me and say I got all of that because I am a prophet of God. That is not correct. He gives it to me because I am a child of God. The office of the prophet is something different, but the gifts of the Spirit are for everybody. When I am moving in the gifts of the Spirit, I am demonstrating what you can do. The gifts of the Spirit are given to every man to profit withal.[1] God wants to use you in detailed ways.

When I say revelation, I am not referring to the book of Revelation or the end time revelation. I am talking about the Spirit of Revelation, His Word being revealed, His will being revealed in your life and the lives of your family. The will of God covers the written as well as the unwritten will. The written will is the Word of God. The unwritten will is what the Holy Spirit wants you to do every day of your life. We need both.

---

[1] 1 Corinthians chapters 12-14

~Living in the Realm of Revelation~

We are desperate to operate in the spirit of revelation. You may not know it, but you are. Without the spirit of revelation, you are in the dark. Without it, you will make many mistakes that will cost you. When you are operating in the spirit of revelation, you will know things that you cannot personally know. You will see things that you cannot naturally see. You will hear things that you cannot naturally hear. You will be able to adjust your life to operate in victory when others are operating in defeat. Can you see the necessity of living in the realm of revelation?

Hosea 4:1; "Hear the word of the LORD, ye children of Israel: for the LORD hath a controversy with the inhabitants of the land, because <u>there is no truth, nor mercy, nor knowledge of God in the land</u>."

Hosea 4:6; "<u>My people are destroyed for lack of knowledge</u>: because thou hast rejected knowledge, I will also reject thee, that thou shalt be no priest to me: seeing thou hast forgotten the law of thy God, I will also forget thy children."

The Hebrew word for knowledge has two Hebrew words connected to it. The first one is *da`ath* (*dah'-ath*). It means to actually gain the knowledge of something. The next Hebrew word is *yada`* (*yaw-dah'*) and it means to perceive something, to gain a revelation of. In other words, to know something that the average person will not know, to perceive something, or to have a revelation of.

God was saying His people were destroyed for a lack of revelation. They didn't have a revelation. You can have head knowledge about God and your life will never change. You have to have an inner knowledge of the mind of Christ and a revelation in your heart, in your spiritual mind about the things of God. That revelation is what will change your life. When you act upon that revelation, follow the full instruction of it you will see your life radically change for the better.

Being destroyed means that things do not work out for you. You get sick and can't get well. You are in poverty and lack and can't prosper. You are defeated and can't walk in victory. Why are we destroyed? It is because of a lack of revelation. Just because you know God wants to heal you doesn't mean you are going to get healed. You have to have a revelation of the healer and what He has already provided for you. You need more than just head knowledge of it or a mental assenting to it.

When revelation comes, manifestation follows. If there is no revelation, there is no manifestation of truth. There has to be a revelation of truth for there to be a manifestation of truth. Catch this with the eyes and ears of your spirit as well as with your heart.

I want to talk about some areas of revelation, that will produce manifestations.

The first one is found in 2 Corinthians 4.

2 Corinthians 4:4-6; "In whom the god of this world hath blinded the minds of them which believe not, lest the light of the glorious gospel of Christ, who is the image of God, should shine unto them. For we preach not ourselves, but Christ Jesus the Lord; and ourselves your servants for Jesus' sake. For God, who commanded the light to shine out of darkness, hath shined in our hearts, to give the light of the knowledge of the glory of God in the face of Jesus Christ."

In these verses there is a revelation of something that is important. If you can catch it, you will understand that the moment someone gets a revelation of salvation, salvation begins to manifest in their life. Satan is very much involved in trying to block revelation from the lost. He does not want the lost to know what Jesus did for them. Paul preaches about the ministry of reconciliation in which God has not imputed the sins of man to them. Jesus paid the price on the cross on Calvary for all sin, past, present and future so that every man is already forgiven. What is the problem then? People don't have a revelation of it and God's people are destroyed for a lack of revelation. We need to know by revelation what Jesus did. The moment you catch and act on that revelation there will be a manifestation of that revelation, of that truth.

Satan wants to stop people from getting and sharing it. He comes with a ministry of condemnation making everybody feel like God hates them. There are people who feel that if they ever walked into a church the building would fall on them. That is a lie.

~Living in the Realm of Revelation~

God is not angry with the sinner. Religion teaches He is and that He wants the sinner to go to hell. If that were true, why would John 3:16-17 have been written?

John 3:16-17; "For God so loved the world, that he gave his only begotten Son, that whosoever believeth in him should not perish, but have everlasting life. For God sent not his Son into the world to condemn the world; but that the world through him might be saved."

The Bible also says that while we were yet sinners Christ died for us. He loves us whether we are a sinner or a saint and has already paid the price for us. You don't have to atone for your own sin. Furthermore, you can't and you can't be good enough to quality for salvation. I remember talking to one man about getting saved. He said that as soon as he got his act together he would come to the Lord. If we never made a mistake, we still wouldn't be good enough. It is not by works of righteousness that we have done, but according to His mercy He saved us. It is all about what Jesus has done on the cross. Because of Adam and Eve, sin has passed through the bloodline to all men. We are all sinners and we all need Jesus. When we come to Him, we are now saints and of the household of faith. [2] You are no longer sinners when you come to Jesus. *"But I still make mistakes."* Saints will. That is why we need to read 1 John 1:9.

1 John 1:9; "If we confess our sins, he is faithful and just to forgive us our sins, and to cleanse us from all unrighteousness."

This scripture was not written to the world but to the church. Jesus made provision for our humanity. I am not trying to sin, but if I do then I can repent of it and know everything will be all right.

<u>The first revelation we need is that Jesus paid the price for our salvation.</u>

The second revelation is found in Matthew 13.

Matthew 13:13-15; "Therefore speak I to them in parables: because they seeing see not; and hearing they hear not, neither do they

---

[2] Ephesians 2

understand. And in them is fulfilled the prophecy of Esaias, which saith, By hearing ye shall hear, and shall not understand; and seeing ye shall see, and shall not perceive: For this people's heart is waxed gross [hard], and their ears are dull of hearing [tired of hearing], and their eyes they have closed; lest at any time they should see with their eyes, and hear with their ears, and should understand with their heart, and should be converted, and I should heal them."

If you can open your spiritual eyes, open your spiritual ears and keep your heart open to God then when revelation comes, you will be delivered, set free and healed. But if you close your eyes, ears and heart to revelation, reject the truth that God is revealing then you won't get healed or set free. Already we are seeing that the revelation is bringing a manifestation if you keep your eyes, ears and heart open.

3 John 1:2-3; "Beloved, I wish above all things that thou mayest prosper and be in health, even as thy soul prospereth. For I rejoiced greatly, when the brethren came and testified of the truth that is in thee, even as thou walkest in the truth."

You will prosper as your soul prospers. Soul in the Greek is *psuche* (*psoo-khay'*) and actually means the spirit, the heart or the spiritual mind. You are going to prosper as you gain the revelation of the truth that Jesus paid for our prosperity at the same time He paid for us to be healed and He paid for our sins. Do you like the thought of prospering and having all your needs met?

I want to show you that Jesus paid for our prosperity on the cross. If He paid for it, then we should receive it because legally it is ours. We can also tell the devil to get His hands off our money.

2 Corinthians 8:9; "For ye know the grace of our Lord Jesus Christ, that, though he was rich, yet for your sakes he became poor, that ye through his poverty might be rich."

When did Jesus become poor? I believe it was when He was on the cross. They stripped Him of everything. He also gave up all the riches of heaven for us when He came to earth. He became the propitiation or a substitute for us. That means what He paid for is legally ours. You have to have a revelation of this in order to rise up in authority and take it back from the devil. Otherwise you will let the devil steal from you and you will think God did it.

When you get a revelation of salvation, salvation comes. Get a revelation of healing and healing comes. Get a revelation of prosperity and prosperity comes.

There is one more area that covers everything else.

2 Peter 1:2-3; "Grace and peace be multiplied unto you through the knowledge of God, and of Jesus our Lord, According as his divine power hath given unto us all things that pertain unto life and godliness, through the knowledge of him that hath called us to glory and virtue:"

Would you like to have grace and peace multiplied in your life? Grace means everything you and I will ever need is gifted to us by God. It is God giving you the abilities you don't have. Healing power is grace. The gifts of the Spirit are grace. To be healed is grace. To be saved is grace. To prosper is grace. Would you like to see an increase of grace because an increase of grace would be an increase of the manifestation of grace. Instead of just being healthy, you would be healthier. Instead of just prospering, you are prospering more. Instead of being used a little by God, you are used by God to a greater degree. The level of grace in your life determines the level of success you walk in.

Years ago, the Holy Spirit told me that not all grace is the same. There is a grace for everything we face. There is saving grace, deliverance grace, healing grace, prosperity grace, and a success grace. There is a grace for your marriage to work, a grace for you to be able to parent your children in a successful way. There is a grace in business, a grace for pastoring churches and for me to travel to the nations. The level of my grace will be the level of my success that I walk in.

Peace is an amazing word. It is tied to the Old Testament words of shalom and shalem. The Greek word is *eirene* (*i-ray'-nay*). It means to be set at one again with God as Adam and Eve were in the Garden. Set at one again, no sin between us and God, no separation between us and God, nothing hindering our one on one relationship. To be totally one with God is this word *eirene*.

Peter said he wanted us to increase in grace and peace. Remember peace is shalom and means nothing missing, broken or lacking.

Would you like to see an increase, a multiplication of grace and peace in your life? Not just an addition but a multiplication. The level of your grace will be the level at which you operate in victory, peace, glory and increase. As your grace increases, so everything else connected to it increases. There is a grace for everything you face. That grace is divine enablement for you to be who you should be and receive what you should receive in order to be a success. Not only is it grace to stand in an office, an anointing, victorious in a business, but also to have all the resource you need to be successful.

How are the grace and peace multiplied? It is through the revelation knowledge of God and of Jesus. The knowledge of God referred to is not talking about head knowledge but about a knowing. It is experiential perception and intimacy. Some have a head knowledge about something, others an experiential knowledge. They have a real revelation and are walking it out. Do you want the experiential knowledge that you are walking out? That is revelation.

So, grace and peace are multiplied according to the revelation that you are walking in. Revelation means an unveiling by the Spirit of God of the fullness and the truth of a thing. God unveils it and makes it real so you can partake of it, walk it out and it becomes yours.

Look again at verse 3.

2 Peter 1:3; "According as his divine power hath given unto us <u>all things</u> that pertain unto life and godliness, through the knowledge of him that hath called us to glory and virtue:"

Things in the Greek really does mean things. Life means anything natural in this life and godliness is anything in the spirit. Knowledge in this verse is speaking about revelation knowledge.

~Living in the Realm of Revelation~

How are we going to get all things that we need in this life and all things we need in the spirit? We get them through revelation by the Spirit of God. We should be living in the realm of revelation. God's will is that you operate fully in that spirit of revelation where the Spirit of God is unveiling things to you about the Word of God and about your life. There are two wills that God wants to unveil to you by the Spirit of Revelation. They are the written will and the unwritten will. We need both.

We need a revelation of the written will of God, which is His Word. The unwritten will answers the questions of what am I supposed to do tomorrow, where I am supposed to live ten years from now, what kind of job am I supposed to take, am I supposed to branch out on my job, am I supposed to have a business and what kind? That is the unwritten will that the Spirit of God wants to reveal.

God can only speak the truth and the devil can only speak lies. Anything you face today that is not in line with the Word of God is a lie from hell and you should reject it viciously. The only truth is God and His Word. Read John 17:17 and John 14:6. Once you get a revelation of authority and truth, you won't put up with anything that is not in line with it. You don't have to because you are the gatekeeper of your life.

Matthew 16:19; "I will give you the keys of the kingdom of heaven [of authority]; and whatever you bind (declare to be improper and unlawful) on earth must be what is already bound in heaven; and whatever you loose (declare lawful) on earth must be what is already loosed in heaven." (Amplified Bible)

You have to already know what is proper in heaven to know what is proper on earth. In other words, you need a revelation of heaven in order to set order in the earth. Is there any sickness in heaven? Do you have a revelation of that? Do you know that in your heart? So, if there is no sickness in heaven, you need to decree that it is unlawful and improper to have sickness on the earth in you. You are the person of authority because you have revelation. You have the keys of the kingdom, which I believe are the keys of revelation.

Someone had a revelation of authority and who God is before Jesus spoke forth this revelation. You will never know who you are until

~Living in the Realm of Revelation~

you know who He is. Who He is determines who you are. As He is so are we in this world. We are children of the Most High God, servants of the Lord, the offspring of God.

Once Peter got a revelation of who Jesus was, Jesus gave him a revelation of who he was. Peter had a revelation that Jesus was the big rock and that determined who Peter was as the little rock. Peter was part of the larger rock.

You need a revelation of who God is before you will ever get a revelation of who you are. If you don't get a revelation of who you are, how are you going to be who you are supposed to be, or how are you going to be a success at anything. It would be like putting a square block in a round hole.

Ever felt like you didn't fit? Part of that is because you didn't know who you are and so you weren't operating in that realm. Can you imagine someone who is not called to be a teacher trying to be one? It won't work and they won't be successful.

It would be like me trying to be a mechanic. I don't fit. I would be a failure and couldn't blame God for it. I would fail in finances and in what I was doing. No one would bring their cars to me. I don't even make a good shade tree mechanic. That is not who I am.

Yet I see God's people trying to operate in realms that are not them. They wonder why they don't prosper and why the blessing of God isn't upon their life. God only blesses you when you fit where you are supposed to fit. A fish can only shine in the water. A bird only has success in the air. Take a fish out of its place, put it on the ground and it will just open its mouth while flopping around. It will have no success and die. Drop that same fish in the water and its genius comes alive.

Some of us need a revelation of who God is and who He made us to be. Then we will be a success in life.

Chapter 2

How to Increase the Power of Revelation In Your Life

In the last chapter, we talked about why we need to operate in the power of revelation and why it is so important. Without a revelation, you can't receive anything from God. If you don't have a revelation that Jesus is the Christ and the only way to heaven, that you are lost and need Him then you can't be saved. You can't be healed until you have a revelation that Jesus is the healer and has already paid the price for you. It can't just be head knowledge, but a heart revelation. Through that you are able to receive.

We also shared about prosperity. Everything you need from God comes through the revelation of what He reveals to you by His Spirit and through His Word.

In this chapter we are going to get into how to increase the power of that revelation. Increase brings increase, so we will be giving you five ways to increase that revelation.

Let me tell you something about God. If you are satisfied with where you are, He will leave you there. He won't increase you until you want increase. He won't even bless you until you want to be blessed. You have to desire healing before healing comes. You have to desire more of God to get more of God.

Proverbs 4:18; "But the path of the just is as the shining light, that shineth more and more unto the perfect day."

Just means the righteous, those who are living for the Lord.

Shining light is speaking about revelation. Anytime you see the word light, it is revelation. Those who are in the dark are in ignorance. The very word light speaks about something revealed. If you turn out all the lights and block all the windows, you would not be able to see what is in a room. Suppose you also didn't know what was in the room, it would then be hard to do anything there without getting hurt. Light brings revelation because you can see. If you can see something, then it is revealed to you. You see what is in the room so you don't walk into a piece of furniture. You are able to function because of sight – revelation.

God doesn't want you to be in the dark because in the dark there is no light. If you can't see then you have no revelation. The path of the just is as a shining light. That path brings revelation that shines more and more. More and more means it is progressive revelation.

When you are driving down a road at night and have your headlights on you can only see as far as you drive. If you are not moving, you will only be able to see a few hundred feet in front of you. Start moving and you will start seeing more. It is the same way in the spirit realm. Revelation is progressive, based upon your moving in God. If you are standing still, you are only going to be able to see just so much. Are you ready to move on in God and do more for the Lord?

Now let's examine the five ways to see the power of revelation increased. What will those five ways do for you? If you get a little bit of revelation about financial breakthrough, you will have a little financial breakthrough. If you get more revelation about a financial breakthrough, you will have a greater financial breakthrough. If you get a little bit of revelation about healing you will see healing begin. If you get a lot of revelation on healing and you will see an overflow of healing come. The level of your revelation is the level of your manifestation.

Increase the Power of Revelation Through the Word

~Living in the Realm of Revelation~

The meditation of the Word, or the Word of God itself, that is taken into your spirit will cause an increase of revelation. Remember, the Word of God is the written will of God.

I want to show you that you have to stay in the Word to receive an increase of revelation. We can't stay away from the Word of God and expect Him to reveal His Word to us. We have to read the Word ourselves, pray and press in everyday. What would happen if e only went to church once a week and listened to the pastor preach? Or what would happen if we only ate one meal a week? Malnutrition and starvation in the answer. Our spirit and or physical bodies would get sick. Neither one can operate like that. They need more sustenance.

Proverbs 6:20-23; "My son, keep thy father's commandment, and forsake not the law of thy mother: Bind them continually upon thine heart, and tie them about thy neck. When thou goest, it shall lead thee; when thou sleepest, it shall keep thee; and when thou awakest, it shall talk with thee. For the commandment is a lamp; and the law is light [revelation]; and reproofs of instruction are the way of life:"

We need to read, study and pray over the Word until it becomes alive in us. Then the manifestation of what is said will begin to happen in us.

Let's say that you begin to read, study and meditate on healing scriptures. You go over and over them every day. Maybe you put them on a CD so you can listen to them over and over. What is going to happen? A revelation and unveiling of one of those verses will take place. What that verse says will start manifesting in your life.

Most people don't understand that if you really want a move of God, really want healing or miracles you are going to have to feed on those scriptures. I call it feed and seed. You have to feed and seed the Word of God deep on the inside of you until you almost overdose. When the revelation of one of those verses comes, it has the power to bring the manifestation of what is revealed.

Psalms 119:105; "Thy [revealed] **word is a lamp unto my feet, and a light unto my path."**

~Living in the Realm of Revelation~

Word in this verse is *dabar* (*daw-baw'*). It means the word revealed. In the Greek, we would be looking at the word *rhema*. *Rhema* is God's Word spoken as if He spoke it for the first time.

Did you know that you can't get somewhere until you know where you are right now? Have you ever called for directions to a certain place and not known exactly where you were right then? No one can give you directions. You have to know where you are.

God's revealed Word will help you locate where you are in God. It will help you locate the level of your faith, what you have and don't have. It will help you locate where you are missing it and where you are hitting it. When you know where you are, then you can find out how to get to where you need to go.

His revealed word is a lamp to my feet so that I can locate myself. It is a light to my path to show me show how to go where I need to go to get where I need to be. The revelation of God's Word does all of this for us.

Psalms 119:130; "The entrance of thy words giveth light; it giveth understanding unto the simple."

You need the entrance of the Word of God. It needs to get from your natural head into your spirit man, into your heart and the mind of your heart. When it gets into the depths of you, it will give light, revelation and understanding unto the simple. It will cause you to be able to receive from God what you need to receive. It will also show you what you need to do. Have you ever been at the point where you really didn't know what to do about your situation?

Psalms 19:7-8; "The law of the LORD is perfect, converting the soul: the testimony of the LORD is sure, making wise the simple. The statutes of the LORD are right, rejoicing the heart: the commandment of the LORD is pure, enlightening the eyes."

Enlightening has to do with revelation. Enlightening the eyes has to do with your spiritual eyes, not your natural ones, giving revelation so you can see what you need to do. The Word of God has the power to give you the information you need. We need to be in the Word.

1 Timothy 4:13-16; "Till I come, give attendance to reading, to exhortation, to doctrine. Neglect not the gift that is in thee, which was given thee by prophecy, with the laying on of the hands of the presbytery. Meditate upon these things; give thyself wholly to them; that thy profiting may appear to all. Take heed unto thyself, and unto the doctrine; continue in them: for in doing this thou shalt both save thyself, and them that hear thee."

Paul starts off by telling Timothy to give attendance to reading the Word of God, exhortation (preaching) and doctrine (teaching of the Word). We need to be hearing preaching and teaching. Many people want to come to a service and have a healing evangelist lay hands on them. That is good, but there is something better.

The reason I say there is something better is because it takes faith for you to stay healed after you get healed. If you don't have enough Word in you because you haven't heard enough teaching, you might get healed but you won't stay healed. I know there are people who think that if you are healed you stay healed.

Have you ever heard of the devil trying to steal someone's healing? The Word says that as soon as the Word is planted the enemy comes to steal it. He comes to steal, kill and destroy because that is his ministry. As a roaring lion seeking whom he may devour, he is doing his stuff. I am not praising him, just saying that he is on the job. If you don't get enough Word in you by hearing good teaching and preaching my faith might get you healed, but it is only your faith that will keep you healed.

Back in the 1940's, 50's and 60's there were many great tent revivals. Masses of people would be healed and masses of people would lose their healing. Some lost it before they ever left the meeting tent. Finally, the preachers and teachers realized they had to change something. They could get the people healed, but the people had no faith to keep their healing. They began teaching the people how to receive and keep their healing. They taught them how to remain healed and what to do if satan tried to steal their healing.

~Living in the Realm of Revelation~

I remember ministering to a man who was scheduled to have knee replacement surgery. When I was finished, I asked him what it was he couldn't do before. He answered that he couldn't go up and down steps. I told him to do it. The man looked at me kind of funny, but went ahead and went up and down the steps. I told him to try and make it hurt. He answered that it wasn't hurting. For two weeks this man was pain free. Then all of a sudden he began hurting worse. He actually went to the doctor and the doctor couldn't find anything wrong even though he was hurting.

The devil will come and try to put that pain back on you so that you will say you guess you didn't get healed. As soon as you say that, he has the right to steal it all from you and return to you all were healed of. He waits for the word of your mouth. You have to watch the words of your mouth. The moment you say you didn't get healed, you have lost that healing. By your words you are justified and by your words you are condemned. If you say, *"By the stripes of Jesus I am healed. He is my healer and I receive my healing"* that is what is going to happen.

This man was taking pain medication and the pain didn't leave. On the way home from the doctor he began to realize that it was the devil trying to steal his healing. He commanded the devil to take the pain and illness and leave in Jesus' name. All the pain left and he never had any more pain.

Many people have told me similar stories. They were healed and several days later the pain tried to return. They rebuked it, told it to leave and they still have their healing. It is not enough to get healed, you have to know how to stay healed. God wants us to get our words in line with our faith and our faith with the Word of God. We need a revelation of the Word of God about healing.

1 Timothy 4:15; "Meditate upon these things; give thyself wholly to them; that thy profiting may appear to all."

Meditate on what you read, what you heard in preaching, what you heard in teaching and on the prophecies that went over your life.

Psalms 1:1-3 Blessed is the man that walketh not in the counsel of the ungodly, nor standeth in the way of sinners, nor sitteth in the seat of the scornful. But his delight is in the law of the LORD; and in his law doth he meditate day and night. And he shall be like a tree planted by the rivers of water, that bringeth forth his fruit in his season; his leaf also shall not wither; and whatsoever he doeth shall prosper."

This is how you will get the full benefit of the Word. Do you want the full benefit and have everything God has for you? Are you spending enough time in the Word? We actually need to take at least one scripture a day and meditate on it all day long. Write it on a little card and carry it with you. Pull it out several times during the day and go over it. Keep feeding on it and thinking about it. What you are reading on that little card is going to happen in your life, but you have to go over it enough to get it from your head to your heart.

Wherever there is a deficiency in your life, there is a scripture for it. Are you facing a physical thing in your life? You need to get hold of some healing scriptures and begin to meditate on at least one of them all day long. Do you need a financial breakthrough? Get some scriptures on it and meditate on them. A scripture a day will keep the devil away. Feed and seed on a scripture that will handle your problem. Instead of complaining about it, do something to change it. Most of us would rather have a solution instead of a problem.

How do you increase the power of revelation? It is through the Word of God.

Increase the Power of Revelation through Praying in Tongues

Romans 8:26-28; "Likewise the Spirit also helpeth our infirmities: for <u>we know not</u> what we should pray for as we ought: but the Spirit itself maketh intercession for us with groanings which cannot be uttered. And <u>He</u> that searcheth the hearts <u>knoweth</u> what is the mind of the Spirit, because he maketh intercession for the saints according to the will of God. <u>And we know</u> that all things work together for good to

~Living in the Realm of Revelation~

them that love God, to them who are the called according to his purpose."

I was preaching this scripture one time and the Holy Spirit stopped me and had me underline these words. He then asked me how it was that we started not knowing and ended up knowing? What is the difference? I knew immediately what it was. Praying in tongues was the answer.

The word "know" is a unique word. The Greek word is *eido* (*i'-do*) meaning <u>to perceive or have a revelation, to see it</u>. So, "not to know" means you have no revelation or can't see it.

All languages have roots in other languages. The New Testament was written in Koine Greek which has its roots in Latin. So, *eido* is actually a Latin word and is from where we get our word video.

I start off with no video, no revelation. I can't see it, but God has the video. He has the revelation. So I pray in tongues. While I am praying I begin to get the video, the revelation and can see it.

We all have spiritual eyes, but they are not active in some of us. Some see in the spirit and don't know they are because they think it is just their imagination. Your imagination was not created by satan but by God. Cell phones, automobiles, washers and dryers, dishwashers, central heating and cooling, electric lights all came from the imagination.

Can we really say the imagination is of the devil? If it is, then we need to get rid of all our appliances, cars, cell phones. Imagination is neither good nor bad. It all depends on how it is used. It is like money. Did you know that money is not evil? The <u>love</u> <u>of</u> <u>money</u> is the root of all evil. Money is a tool, neither good nor bad. In the hands of a child of God it can buy an orphanage, pay off a church, feed the hungry, clothe the naked, and send out a missionary. In the hands of a drug dealer it can destroy lives. It is all based on the heart of the person.

The same thing is true of imagination. A sanctified imagination can be used as a mighty tool. If you sanctify it enough, the Holy Ghost can slip a video in on you and show you past, present and future in high definition. Sometimes it happens when I minister to people. God can take me back to an accident they had ten or twenty years ago. I can see it color, how the vehicles collided and what happened to the people. How can that happen? If you sanctify your imagination then God can use it.

Are you ready for God to use your imagination for His glory? Maybe He will give you an invention that will change the world.

How do you sanctify your imagination? It is by casting down vain imaginations, any high thing that exalts itself against the knowledge of God, bringing into captivity every thought to the obedience of Christ. In other words, you have to be the director and the producer of the videos. Join hands with God.

The movies I am going to have upon the screen of my spirit will be my healing, my prosperity, the scriptures coming alive, and the stories in the Word of God being played. I have to be the director of that. If the video goes astray, I am going to stop it. I will rebuke and command it to leave. The quicker you are to direct your imagination in the right direction, the quicker the Holy Spirit will begin to use it for your benefit and the benefit of others.

Have you ever researched the word meditate in either the Old or New Testament? In the rendering of the meaning you will find the word imagine. You are supposed to imagine God's Word working. You are supposed to read in the Word that by the stripes of Jesus you are healed and then see yourself healed.

We are supposed to be producing the video of God's Word upon the imagination of our hearts. When we do, we sanctify it and block any evil imagination. God even said at the tower of Babel that whatever they imagine to do, they will be able to. Are you ready to restore your imagination. It is the creative part of God that He gave you and satan wants to corrupt it that is has no power to produce good for you. We need to cleanse our imagination through the Blood and the Word of God and begin to produce the right videos upon our imagination.

When we pray more in tongues a spirit of revelation will begin to operate.

~Living in the Realm of Revelation~

1 Corinthians 2:12-13; "Now we have received, not the spirit of the world, but the spirit which is of God; that we might know the things that are freely given to us of God. Which things also we speak, not in the words which man's wisdom teacheth, but which the Holy Ghost teacheth; comparing spiritual things with spiritual."

This is speaking about revelation. The Spirit of God comes so we can know.

I heard one noted preacher say that verse 13 is about speaking in tongues. The words which man teaches is our birth language or the language we grew up speaking. There is another language called the heavenly language that is taught to you by the Holy Ghost. Through the Holy Spirit we can know those things that are freely given to us by God. We can know what is supposed to be ours and get a revelation of it. <u>If you get a revelation of it you will have a manifestation of it.</u>

1 Corinthians 14:2; "For he that speaketh in an unknown tongue speaketh not unto men, but unto God: for no man understandeth him; howbeit in the spirit he speaketh mysteries."

Mysteries means divine secrets or things/revelations that God has that we don't have. So when we are praying in tongues we are praying divine secrets, revelations that God has and we don't. Why is that important? It is because while you are praying it out you are praying the complete solution to every problem you are facing.

Jesus never prayed the problem. Read John 17. He always prayed the solution. When you pray in tongues you are praying the solution, the answer. It is a prayer that will always be answered because it is the perfect prayer. It is the will of God.

1 Corinthians 14:14-15; "For if I <u>pray</u> in an unknown tongue, my spirit prayeth, but my understanding is unfruitful. What is it then? I will pray with the spirit, and I will pray with the understanding also: I will sing with the spirit, and I will sing with the understanding also."

Verse 14 doesn't say speak or say. It says pray. There is a prayer language.

There are three things people get mixed up on. First- there is the initial receiving tongue which you get when you are filled with the Holy Spirit and start speaking in tongues. Then- there is the devotional tongue you use when you pray in tongues. Lastly- there is a message in tongues that should be interpreted. Not everything you pray in tongues should be interpreted. Some things are only to God and that is what verse 2 says. When you pray in an unknown tongue you are not praying to men but unto God. If I am praying to God why do you need to know what it is? You don't.

I also know that when I pray with people from different denominations, I won't pray in tongues with them. They wouldn't understand what I was going to say or what I was doing and it would offend them. So, I would pray in English with them. We would take turns praying for each other. When I get together with people who understand praying in tongues and do it we can all pray in tongues together. There is a time to do it and a time not to do it. I have also learned how to pray in tongues under my breath and hardly anyone knows what I am saying or doing.

Verse 14 doesn't say my flesh or natural mind prays. It says my spirit prays but my understanding is unfruitful. Understanding can also mean interpretation or revelation. There are times when I will ask the Holy Spirit what I was praying in tongues about. The understanding will just come to me.

Communing with the Holy Spirit

If you pray a lot in tongues, you need to learn how to commune with the Holy Spirit.

2 Corinthians 13:14; "The grace of the Lord Jesus Christ, and the love of God, and the communion of the Holy Ghost, be with you all. Amen."

Communion is the Greek word *koinonia*. *Koinonia* has to do with communication, distribution, and partnership.

~Living in the Realm of Revelation~

John 16:13-14; "Howbeit when he, the Spirit of truth, is come, he will guide you into all truth: for he shall not speak of himself; but whatsoever he shall hear, that shall he speak: and he will shew you things to come. He shall glorify me: for he shall receive of mine, and shall shew it unto you."

This speaks of revelation. He is revealing and unveiling.

John 16:15; "All things that the Father hath are mine: therefore said I, that he shall take of mine, and shall shew it unto you."

Unveil means to show or reveal it so you can receive, see and take hold of it.

Let me show you what communing with the Holy Spirit is and connect it to prayer in tongues. Let's say you have been praying in tongues for a while. It is okay to ask the Holy Spirit what you have been saying in tongues. What does it hurt to ask? If He doesn't want to tell you He won't, but what if He wants to?

I remember one time when I felt an unction to function in tongues. It was a pull to go ahead and pray in tongues over something. I got caught up and later realized it was over two hours. It had felt like ten minutes. I asked the Holy Spirit what I had been praying about. Then I saw the face of a lady pastor in Texas in a flash vision. You could say I saw it in my mind's eye or my imagination. I knew it had something to do with her. Next, I saw the church building in a flash vision. I had total peace that everything was okay. I hadn't seen this pastor for two years. I called her a couple of days later and told her that I had been praying in tongues for about two hours. I went on to say I asked the Holy Spirit about it and I saw her face and the church building. Then I asked her what was going on.

She told me they had found some sort of growth on her vocal cords. She had worn out and destroyed them. She would have to quit the ministry because she wouldn't be able to preach anymore. I asked about the building. There was a balloon payment due in 3 days and they didn't have the money. The building would be foreclosed on if they didn't pay. I told her she would be okay and they would not lose the church building.

~Living in the Realm of Revelation~

A year later I realized I hadn't heard anything so I called. She told me she was healed and well, preaching every service. The church building was also paid off.

Move in that power of revelation and commune with the Holy Spirit. Ask the Holy Spirit questions. He is our helper. One of the words for helper is parakletos. It means one who goes along side to help us. It also means a teacher, a counselor, a guide. If He is your teacher, aren't you supposed to ask a teacher questions?

We have the Holy Spirit as our helper and we are not using Him. You have not because you don't ask.[3] A man came to me one time and asked why God showed me people's names, illnesses and problems. I told him it was because I asked Him to. With a blank look on his face, he asked if we could really do that. He didn't think we could.

It is not just our thinking, we need a revelation of the Word of God. A lot of what we think is wrong and is keeping us in lack. Are you ready to break out of lack and go into the blessings of the Lord? I want the fullness of what God has for me.

Several years ago I was at a conference and learned that when a ministry is powerful it is because of prayer. The ministry doing the conference had a prayer team of three hundred intercessors. Their church had morning prayer and a different pastor would lead it each day. One morning, the leading pastor asked for any other pastors to join him and help lead the meeting. He led the first prayer and I came next. I was used to communing with the Holy Spirit so I asked Him to show me details, names, illnesses about people and I would do whatever He wanted me to.

I look down and saw a woman. Instantly I knew she had a loved one in jail. I heard the name John. The prayer meeting got started and I was given the microphone. I began by saying that a woman there was very concerned about a loved one. His name was John. I then said her right leg was damaged. She answered it was and she needed it healed. The power of

---

[3] James 4:2

God hit the whole place at once. We began laying hands on people and everyone was healed.

You can do the same thing, just learn to commune with the Holy Ghost. You can be on a job interview, commune with the Holy Ghost and know exactly what to say and do to get the job. The Holy Spirit may tell you that you don't want that job so don't say much. They will cheat you and not pay very well. You are going to that interview with the Holy Spirit and it is all on the inside of you.

There is a conversation going on between God and me when I am ministering to people. When I get quiet it is because I am communing with the Holy Spirit. On the inside of me there is a conversation going on. I am asking the Spirit of the Lord what I should do, asking Him to show me the next thing, asking what something means.

The Holy Spirit is not offended by your questions unless you are questioning Him out of fear, doubt and unbelief. Mary questioned the Holy Spirit.[4] She wasn't asking in the wrong way. The angel told her it was simple, the Holy Ghost would come upon her. Zacharias also questioned but out of unbelief. The angel came along and smote his mouth so he couldn't speak and ruin everything.

There is a question that is a right question and a question that is a wrong question. If it is out of fear, doubt and unbelief then keep your mouth shut. If there is something you want to know so you can operate more with the Holy Ghost, then ask it.

How to Increase the Power of Revelation

You increase the power of revelation by praying for it. Again we refer to James 4:2. You have not because you ask not.

Ephesians 1:16-19; "Cease not to give thanks for you, making mention of you in my prayers; That the God of our Lord Jesus Christ, the Father of glory, may give unto you the spirit of wisdom and

---

[4] Luke 1

revelation in the knowledge of him: The eyes of your understanding being enlightened; that ye may know what is the hope of his calling, and what the riches of the glory of his inheritance in the saints, And what is the exceeding greatness of his power to us-ward who believe, according to the working of his mighty power,"

Verse 17 says that our Lord gave us the spirit of wisdom and revelation in the knowledge of him. Paul was praying for the church of Ephesus to have the spirit of revelation. You can pray for yourself to have that spirit of revelation. We need to be praying that prayer quite often.

Be People who are Generous

Generosity is not about how much money you have.

T.D. Jakes uses an example that I like. He asked what if there is a man, a hobo living on the streets who had no money at all. As he is walking along the street, he finds an apple. He sees his friend and offers him half of the apple. That is generosity.

What about a couple of bag ladies on the street? One of them finds a sack of clothes. She finds some other ladies and shares the clothes with all of them. They can take what they want and she will take the rest. That is generosity.

God will test you with money to see if He can trust you with His revelations, with His glory, anointing and power. If you are not a giver, He will never trust with greater riches.

Luke 16:10-11; "He that is faithful in that which is least is faithful also in much: and he that is unjust in the least is unjust also in much. If therefore ye have not been faithful in the unrighteous mammon, who will commit to your trust the true riches?"

In His wisdom, God says that if you are faithful in a little thing He can trust you with big things. If you are not faithful with unrighteous mammon (things) how can He trust you with the true riches?

Chapter 3

Revelation Gifts

The revelation power that reveals the Word of God will also reveal other things that you need to know. In this chapter we will be talking about the gifts of the Spirit and the three categories of the gifts.

1 Corinthians 12:7-11; "But the manifestation of the Spirit is given to every man to profit withal. For to one is given by the Spirit the word of wisdom; to another the word of knowledge by the same Spirit; To another faith by the same Spirit; to another the gifts of healing by the same Spirit; To another the working of miracles; to another prophecy; to another discerning of spirits; to another divers kinds of tongues; to another the interpretation of tongues: But all these worketh that one and the selfsame Spirit, dividing to every man severally as he will."

There are nine manifestations (some call them gifts) of the Holy Spirit. All of these manifestations are in the Holy Spirit and if you are a born again Spirit-filled believer, the Holy Spirit is in you. If you will learn how to yield to the Holy Spirit and the Spirit of Revelation those manifestations will flow through you as they are needed. But you have to understand how it works.

We are going to put the manifestations into three different categories. There are the gifts of utterance. These are the <u>gifts that say something</u> and they are prophecy, tongues and interpretation of tongues. Then there are the <u>gifts that do something</u> and they are the gift of faith, the working of miracles and the gifts of healings. Lastly, there are the <u>gifts</u>

that reveal or unveil something. These are the word of knowledge, the word of wisdom and the discerning of spirits.

I want to focus on the three gifts that reveal something. These are the revelation gifts and we are going to tie them into the spirit of revelation. The Holy Spirit is called the Spirit of Revelation. One of His main ministries is to reveal things to us about God and what God has prepared for us.

John 16:13-15; "Howbeit when he, the Spirit of truth, is come, he will guide you into all truth: for he shall not speak of himself; but whatsoever he shall hear, that shall he speak: and he will shew you things to come. He shall glorify me: for he shall receive of mine, and shall shew [disclose, unveil or to reveal] **it unto you. All things that the Father hath are mine: therefore said I, that he shall take of mine, and shall shew it unto you."**

All three of these verses say that the Holy Spirit is the spirit of truth that unveils or reveals things about God and things that God has for us. It can even be things in the past, present or future, about the Word of God or things that are about our lives.

Ephesians 1:16-17; "Cease not to give thanks for you, making mention of you in my prayers; That the God of our Lord Jesus Christ, the Father of glory, may give unto you the spirit of wisdom and revelation in the knowledge of him:"

Paul is calling the Holy Spirit the spirit of wisdom and revelation. He is there to reveal things to us.

Romans 8:26-28; "So too the [Holy] Spirit comes to our aid *and* bears us up in our weakness; for we do not know what prayer to offer *nor* how to offer it worthily as we ought, but the Spirit Himself goes to meet our supplication *and* pleads in our behalf with unspeakable yearnings *and* groanings too deep for utterance. And He Who searches the hearts of men knows what is in the mind of the [Holy] Spirit [what His intent is], because the Spirit intercedes *and* pleads [before God] in behalf of the saints according to *and* in harmony with God's will." Amplified Bible

Now, we are going to talk about the written and the unwritten will of God. We know the written will is our Bible, the Word of God. The unwritten will concerns things about your personal life. You will not find it in the Bible that you are supposed to move to a certain city and live on a certain street. It won't name the company you are supposed to work for. That is the unwritten will. You have to understand that the Holy Spirit wants to unveil the will of God, meaning the written will and the unwritten will. In the spirit of revelation He wants to do that.

Next, I want to look at Romans 12:1-2. Many of us know this verse, but sometimes we think we know but we really don't know it as well as we should. Because the Holy Spirit is always reveling and unveiling more.

Romans 12:1-2; "I beseech you therefore, brethren, by the mercies of God, that ye present your bodies a living sacrifice, holy, acceptable unto God, which is your reasonable service. And be not conformed to this world: but be ye transformed by the renewing of your mind, that ye may prove what is that good, and acceptable, and perfect, will of God."

You need to know both parts of God's will - the written as well as the unwritten. The unwritten will that you are receiving from the Lord must come in line with the written will. If the unwritten will that you seem to be receiving is not in line with the written will, it is the wrong information.

First and foremost, you want to stay with the revelation of the written will. Then judge everything else you receive according to the revelation of the written will. If you do and you are getting information that is either scripture or scriptural and is in line with the Word then you know it is the correct information. Everything you receive in the spirit you must judge according to the revelation of the written will of God. We teach this in the School of the Prophets.[5]

---

[5] For more information on the School of the Prophets, please visit our website: www.prophetphilrich.com

~Living in the Realm of Revelation~

John 14:17; "Even the Spirit of truth; whom the world cannot receive, because it seeth him not, neither knoweth him: but ye know him; for he dwelleth with you, and shall be in you."

I want you to understand where the Spirit of Revelation is. If you are a born again Spirit filled believer, where is the Spirit of God in connection to you? He is living on the inside of you. Christ in you, the hope of glory.[6]

So, how far away is the Spirit of Revelation? He is closer than the breath you breathe. He is living on the inside of you. So, from where will He bring revelation to you? It will be from the inside of you. That is why you have to learn how to monitor where the voices are coming from. If it is a bubble up, then it is the Holy Spirit. The Old Testament word for prophecy was bubble up. In the Old Testament the prophets, priests and kings could be filled with the Holy Spirit and have Him working in and on them. Under the New Covenant because of the day of Pentecost and what Jesus did on the cross we now have the Holy Spirit residing on the inside of us when we receive Jesus as Lord and Savior.

As we begin to speak about the Spirit of Revelation, I want to talk about four things and how He deals with us as well as how He speaks to us. We will begin in 1 Corinthians 2 and talk about the Spirit revealing and how He so desires to reveal things to us.

1 Corinthians 2:9-10; "But as it is written, Eye hath not seen, nor ear heard, neither have entered into the heart of man, the things which God hath prepared for them that love him. But God hath revealed them unto us by his Spirit: for the Spirit searcheth all things, yea, the deep things of God."

I believe the Holy Spirit can reveal person, places and things to us.

1 Corinthians 2:12; "Now we have received, not the spirit of the world, but the spirit which is of God; that we might know the things that are freely given us of God."

---

[6] Colossians 1:27

~Living in the Realm of Revelation~

You and I have the Spirit of Revelation living on the inside of us and He is willing at all times to reveal. I believe Father God is sitting on a throne and Jesus, the Son is seated next to Him. But the Spirit of God is living within the believer. Not only does the Spirit reveal, but we also have the spirit of revelation. This is the second thing.

1 Corinthians 2:13; "Which things also we speak, not in the words which man's wisdom teacheth, but which the Holy Ghost teacheth; comparing spiritual things with spiritual."

A noted woman teacher said this verse refers to speaking in tongues. I believe she is right. In the natural, man taught us to speak a natural language. This verse says the Holy Ghost is teaching us another language. In other words, we have received a language taught to us by the Holy Ghost. When we pray in tongues, we are comparing spiritual things with spiritual. We are discerning what is God and what isn't.

If we truly want to operate in the spirit of revelation, we need to be people who pray in tongues every day. There are prayer muscles that you will develop. When you pray in tongues, you are activating the spirit of revelation.

1 Corinthians 14:2; "For he that speaketh in an unknown tongue speaketh not unto men, but unto God: for no man understandeth him; howbeit in the spirit he speaketh mysteries."

Mysteries means divine secrets, things that God knows and we don't. Isn't it amazing that when you pray in tongues you are praying mysteries, divine secrets. You are praying the answer instead of the problem, the solution instead of the trouble you are going through. The Bible tells us that we can even find out what we are praying in tongues about.

1 Corinthians 14:14-15; "For if I pray in an unknown tongue, my spirit prayeth, but my understanding is unfruitful. What is it then? I will pray with the spirit, and I will pray with the understanding also: I will sing with the spirit, and I will sing with the understanding also."

~Living in the Realm of Revelation~

Your spirit praying is better than just your natural man praying. The Amplified Bible says that your spirit by the Holy Spirit within you prays. You and the Holy Ghost are working together in intimate communion.

Understanding means you get the understanding of what you were praying in tongues. If you pray enough in tongues, you will operate more in the word of knowledge, word of wisdom and discerning of spirits. You may experience a bubble up effect. Sometimes it comes in the way of a flash vision. He may give you a name, situation, a knowing in your imagination.

So, you can pray with the spirit and pray with the understanding or pray with the interpretation. Many times it comes as a knowing. Once you are activated in this and doing it all the time you are hooked up and can go about your day communing with God.

The fourth thing is that we can receive instruction from the Holy Spirit. The first was that the Spirit God reveals. The second was that we have the Spirit of Revelation on the inside of us. Third, we can pray in tongues and stir up the spirit of revelation. Lastly, we can receive the instruction from the Spirit of Revelation.

1 Corinthians 2:14-16; "But the natural man receiveth not the things of the Spirit of God: for they are foolishness unto him: neither can he know them, because they are spiritually discerned [received, understood]. **But he that is spiritual judgeth all things, yet he himself is judged of no** [fleshly] **man. For who hath known the mind of the Lord, that he may instruct him? But we have the mind of Christ."**

Carnal people who don't know God can't figure you out. No man can judge you in the flesh because you are in the spirit. Someone in the flesh can't judge somebody who is in the spirit. They will get it all wrong. You have to be spiritual to discern somebody spiritual.

The mind of Christ is activated by the spirit of revelation. The Holy Spirit unveils the written will and the unwritten will and then we take on the mind of Christ so we can receive instruction from Him.

~Living in the Realm of Revelation~

Ways That We Receive This Revelation

The first way that you receive a knowing of something or knowings. You find in 1 Corinthians 2:14 & 16.

There are things I call knowings. You just know, but don't know how you know because nobody in the flesh told you. There have been times when I have been around someone and they didn't tell me a thing, yet I knew things about them. We call that knowings. It is actually a word of knowledge.

A word of knowledge, word of wisdom and discerning of spirits can come by knowings. If you pray enough in tongues all of a sudden, you will know something. You know what is happening tomorrow, know things about people, places and about things. Not knowing how you know them, you must think it has to be God. The Spirit of Revelation is causing you to know what you cannot know. Sometimes it is so real that you think somebody told you. I have actually asked people if they had told me. Many of them didn't and yet I know it. People have even told me they haven't told anybody. So, sometimes you can receive special revelation by the knowings.

Another way of receiving can be by impressions that come.

Acts 18:5; "And when Silas and Timotheus were come from Macedonia, Paul was pressed [impressed] in the spirit, and testified to the Jews that Jesus was Christ."

He got an impression that he should testify, what to say and what to do.

An impression is an inner working. It is actually an unction to function from the inside out. You know you ought to do it. That is an impression. You know what you should say and don't know how you know it except you feel it inside.

There is an impression you should give in an offering, tell someone about Jesus, share a testimony or that you need to say something. It could be an impression that you need to intercede or get into the Word. This is moving into the revelatory realm, the realm of revelation.

The next way is called leadings. You feel a leading to do something.

Romans 8:14; "For as many as are led by the Spirit of God, they are the sons of God."

I heard one minister say that a leading is like a boat with a sail and the wind blowing on the sail leading the boat.

Sometimes God will lead us and we don't even know it. We are prompted to go a direction. It is so light and gentle that it feels like a soft breeze. We can go against it if we want to. We are led to go a different route on our trip and avoid an accident. We are led to do something different in our routine one particular day and it spares us and our family.

Don't let locked into doing the same thing every day. Let the Holy Spirit deviate it for you if necessary. I have learned something about satan. He knows your routine and he sets you up for a snare. Learn to be led by the Spirit.

God never drives us. He leads us. He prompts us gently. God will also bear witness with our spirit.

Romans 8:16; "The Spirit itself beareth witness with our spirit, that we are the children of God:"

This scripture doesn't say He bears witness with our head or our body. He bears witness with our spirit that we are the children of God.

Bear witness means to let your spirit know something is right or something is wrong. I believe the Holy Spirit wants to lead us this way more than we even imagine. Most of the time He is going to bear witness with you, gently lead you. Your head and your body will say that they don't think it is God, but your spirit will know it is.

~Living in the Realm of Revelation~

Some will say it is like a velvety feeling on the inside. It is not a physical feeling but a spiritual one. Your spirit man has feelings.

If it feels like in the spirit that you are putting a glove on the wrong hand and it just doesn't feel right, that is the bearing witness. We know how it feels when a shoe fits just right. That is how it is in the spirit when He bears witness with us. It is not physical. It is spiritual, on the inside of you.

Conscience is still another way.

Romans 9:1; "I say the truth in Christ, I lie not, my conscience also bearing me witness in the Holy Ghost,"

Do you understand what it is to have your conscience hurt? If you know you are supposed to do something and you go against it, you will hurt. It will usually hurt right in your center. Your conscience is not of your mind. It is of your spiritual mind, of your heart.

Have you ever done something you knew inside you were supposed to do? You were excited. Your conscience was happy, ready to have a party. It felt so good on the inside because you did the right thing and followed the Holy Spirit. You gave that offering He told you to, helped that family or took food to those who had none. You did what you were supposed to do and on the inside your conscience is being rewarded by the Holy Ghost.

Just disobey God about something and see how your conscience feels. It will almost feel like a stomach ache. You can hurt on the inside of your conscience. I have been where I couldn't even sleep at night because my conscience was bothering me. I had to get up and tell the Lord that when the sun came up I was taking care of it. I would and as soon as I did, the party on the inside started.

Now let's talk about seeing something on the big screen of your spirit as well as hearing something in the spirit.

Acts 10:3-6; "He saw in a vision evidently about the ninth hour of the day an angel of God coming in to him, and saying unto him,

Cornelius. And when he looked on him, he was afraid, and said, What is it, Lord? And he said unto him, Thy prayers and thine alms are come up for a memorial before God. And now send men to Joppa, and call for one Simon, whose surname is Peter: He lodgeth with one Simon a tanner, whose house is by the sea side: he shall tell thee what thou oughtest to do."

Cornelius is not only seeing, he is hearing. It is amazing how many times when I seeing, I will also hear something particularly if it gets my attention and I am listening.

Have you ever noticed all the details Cornelius received? It wasn't something like someone has a toe ache. It was deeper than that.

Cornelius got the name of the city, the two parts of Peter's name, who Peter was staying with, what the occupation of that man was, where this man lived and what Peter would tell Cornelius.

I remember going into one church several years ago and ministering to a lady. I mentioned the name Mary and she said that was her name. I talked about the three children that she prayed for. The Holy Spirit was giving me a lot of information about Mary. I went to another lady and said there were three chapters in the Bible that she read constantly and she loved them more than anything. She opened up a piece of paper and showed me those three chapters. It was exactly what I had said. I ministered to another family and said a PO Box number. They said it was theirs. I went on to say they were waiting for a check. Yes, they were. Then I told them it was going to arrive soon. God was moving in that service.

The people in that church had never seen me do that and they said I was a psychic, as if the devil is greater than God. They went on to say it was not of God and the pastor agreed with them because he had never seen anything like that. He was a Pentecostal pastor of a church that had over five hundred people.

I was there to preach in a convention. My message was titled "What Can God Reveal". I used chapters 9 and 10 of Acts and went through the details. Afterwards, this pastor came up to me and said he needed to see me privately. We went off to the side and this man cried on my shoulder. He said he didn't know all of that. No one had ever taught it. If fact, he had even talked against me and had put me down because he didn't know God could do that. Imagine, someone who had pastored for almost twenty years and he didn't know what God could do. He didn't know because he had never been taught. No one ever told him and no one ever moved in that kind of power.

My job is to impart the gifts of the Spirit and activate your eyes, ears and spirit. I can't give you the office of a prophet because only God can do that, but I can definitely impart the ability for you to move in all nine gifts of the Spirit with accuracy and power. I can do that and God wants me to. We need to be moving in the power and glory of God in today's world. The written will and unwritten will must be revealed. It is time for God's people to come out of the dark and come into the light of God. It takes an unveiling and a coming together of the fivefold ministry.

God wants us to be people who can stand up secure and strong, doing what needs to be done, taking care of business. Yes, we have a sensitive side, have the fruit of the Spirit, but we will not put up with devils and evil.

God also wants us to hear.

There is a wonderful story in 1 Kings 19. It occurred during a time when the prophet was discouraged. Have you ever had a moment of discouragement?

In the following verses we see that God wants to give the prophet another lesson in hearing His voice.

1 Kings 19:11-12; "And he said, Go forth, and stand upon the mount before the LORD. And, behold, the LORD passed by, and a great and strong wind rent the mountains, and brake in pieces the rocks before the LORD; but the LORD was not in the wind: and after the wind an earthquake; but the LORD was not in the earthquake: And after the earthquake a fire; but the LORD was not in the fire: and after the fire a still small voice."

~Living in the Realm of Revelation~

Most of the time when God talks to me it is gently on the inside of me. If God has to boom from heaven, you are in trouble. Study it in the Bible. Every time God had to speak loudly from heaven, He was straightening somebody out. He was dealing with fear, doubt and unbelief, with people who were obstinate against Him. You don't want God booming His voice from heaven because it means He is not happy with you. You want Him speaking softly and gently on the inside of you where the Holy Ghost dwells in the heart of man. You want Him speaking in a gentle, soft voice a scripture that just bubbles up in the night and fits your situation. Maybe while you are praying in tongues softly, meditating on the Lord He is sweetly encourages from the inside out.

Do you want the Spirit of Revelation to work in your life? Do you want to operate in words of knowledge, words of wisdom and discerning of spirits? If you will operate in the spirit of revelation, it should be easy for you to catch it. The Lord doesn't want to make it hard to hear His voice and follow Him. It is so simple that we would have to complicate it in order to miss what He wants to say to us. It starts by just believing what it says in the written word. *"God lives on the inside of me. His Spirit is on the inside of me. Christ in me the hope of glory. He is speaking to me right now."*

Chapter 4

Revelation Secrets

We have been talking about how to live in the realm of revelation where the Holy Spirit unveils things to us so that we are not in the dark about anything

There are eight revelation secrets I want to share with you. They will help you to better yield yourself to the revelation power of the Holy Spirit in your daily life so that you can know things. God doesn't want you to be blind, ignorant or caught unaware about anything. The Holy Spirit is called the Spirit of Revelation and the Spirit of Truth. He will guide us into all truth.

The word truth in the Greek means <u>verity or reality as God know it</u>. We have a natural reality that is not really reality because it can change. That is why truth is such an awesome thing. Real truth cannot change. Truth is constant, forever the same. That is how you know it is truth. This why Jesus and His Word are truth. God cannot change. He is the same today, yesterday and forever.[7] Same in the Greek is *autos* (*ow-tos'*) meaning identically the same. He is the same in His love, purpose and personality as well as His way of doing things and touching our lives. His purposes have never changed. His message of salvation has never changed. It is all about Jesus. In fact, every book of the bible points to Jesus Christ.

---

[7] Hebrews 13:8

~Living in the Realm of Revelation~

There are secrets in every realm of life. A secret can give you the edge. If you are a finished carpenter, there are secrets some finished carpenters know that gives them the edge and they are a step above the others. It is the same way in plumbing and electrical work. We find it with those who are artists. There is a certain way to do brush strokes and mix paint that makes their artwork better than anyone else's. It is true in every facet of life.

The Holy Ghost has secrets. I can hear someone say that there are no secrets, but that is not what the Bible says.

Proverbs 3:32; "... but his [the Lord's] **secret is with the righteous."**

God doesn't tell everybody everything. He tells certain people certain things and some have privileged information. Have you positioned yourself for privileged information? There are confidential things in the government that they just don't tell the common person. I want to release some top secret information to you.

Isaiah 11:1-4; "And there shall come forth a rod out of the stem of Jesse, and a Branch shall grow out of his roots: And the spirit of the LORD shall rest upon him, the spirit of wisdom and understanding, the spirit of counsel and might, the spirit of knowledge and of the fear of the LORD; And shall make him of quick understanding in the fear of the LORD: and he shall not judge [discern] **after the sight of his eyes, neither reprove after the hearing of his** [natural] **ears: But with righteousness shall he judge** [discern] **the poor, and reprove with equity for the meek of the earth: and he shall smite the earth with the rod of his mouth, and with the breath of his lips shall he slay the wicked."**

This is a prophecy about the sevenfold anointing on Jesus. Jesus learned to operate not by natural things, but by supernatural things. We have to move into the realm where we are not trying to do supernatural things naturally. Jesus operated spiritually from the realm of the spirit.

Did you know that you have spiritual eyes and natural eyes? You also have spiritual ears and natural ears. There is a natural part of you and a supernatural part of you. Your flesh is the natural part. Stop trying to discern the things of God with your natural man. Quit trying to discern Him with your thoughts. Don't look at something and say it is different from what you are used to so it must be of the devil. That is not righteous discernment.

I have found out that sometimes God moves in a way I am not used to Him moving, but that doesn't mean it isn't Him. It just means I am not used to it. Suppose you go into a meeting and there is gold dust falling all over people and you are not used to seeing that in a church setting. If you go by your natural mind you will say that can't be right. Go into places where people are shaking and falling to the floor and your natural mind will say something is wrong. Yet God is moving, lives are being changed and people are getting saved.

We have to quit discerning after our natural mind, our natural senses and trying to decide from the natural what is spiritual and what isn't. Jesus did not discern after the sight of His natural eyes. Neither did He discern after the hearing of His natural ears, but He did righteous discernment. There have been times I have missed it because I was looking at something I wasn't used to and misjudged it. That is easy to do if you go by the natural, by what you are used to.

"Well, I am used to people getting the Holy Ghost in one particular way. If they get it any other way, I don't know how to handle that." "I am used to God healing people in a certain way with the laying on of hands. If it doesn't happen with the laying on of hands, I don't know how to handle that." God knows how to heal in a thousand ways and He is not going to get stuck in your or my box. He won't stay in the box. He will go somewhere else where people won't tell Him there is only one way He can move, save, heal and deliver. God has ways we don't even know about yet.

Perception

One of the revelatory secrets is that you have to come to the place where you perceive from the realm of the spirit. Perception in the spirit is not about anything natural. It is about everything spiritual. It is something you do in the spirit realm, not the natural one. You can't look at the natural and perceive anything. I have been in churches where the people have tried to discern me. They will look at me, trying to find out where I am coming from. You can't discern me with the natural when I am teaching or ministering because I am not operating in the natural. I am operating in the spirit so you have to discern me in the spirit, according to the Word of God, according to the Spirit of God and how God speaks.

Each of us have personal preferences for the type of ministry we will go hear and see. Some prefer loud demonstrative preaching. That is only one way of ministering. Sometimes we need to sit down and have a teacher teach us the Word of God. It is not about emotions, but it will give you emotions when you understand the revelation that is coming forth.

Matthew 4:23-24 tells us that Jesus went everywhere teaching, preaching and healing all manner of sickness and disease. He taught first, then preached and proclaimed it. Explanation, proclamation and then demonstration. We need all three. If all you have is preaching, you get people excited but they are not stable, grounded in the Word of God. They will be flighty and emotional. When the devil attacks them and they don't feel tingles going up and down their spine then they think they have lost it. When you are grounded in the Word of God, nothing moves you. Whether you feel it or not, you know what God's Word says and that is so. The Word of God will stabilize you. It will keep you solid when satan is hitting you with everything.

I can teach God's Word and get so excited that I want to jump and dance, shout and run. There are times when I am staying in a hotel and studying that the Word jumps off the page and into my heart. At those times, I have to jump and dance a little bit. I might even do a little yelling out. Then I usually check the clock to see what time it is because I don't want to bother anyone who is in a room around me. I wasn't just dancing and jumping for emotion. It was because of revelation. The truth of God's Word came alive on the inside of me.

We need to change what we get emotional about. Our emotions have to be trained. You are responsible for your emotions and have to train them by the Word of God, by the Spirit of God so they don't rule you. You need to rule them. No matter if you do or don't feel saved, you are because the Word of God says you are saved so you tell your emotions to get in line with the Word. It doesn't matter what your day may be like, you still have the victory whether you feel it or not, whether circumstances dictate it or not. The Word of God in you will dictate the circumstances and command them to come in line.

Matthew 13:13-15; "Therefore speak I to them in parables: because they seeing see not; and hearing they hear not, neither do they understand. And in them is fulfilled the prophecy of Esaias, which saith, By hearing ye shall hear, and shall not understand; and seeing ye shall see, and shall not <u>perceive</u>: For this people's heart is waxed gross, and their ears are dull of hearing, and their eyes they have closed; lest at any time they should see with their eyes, and hear with their ears, and should understand with their heart, and should be converted, and I should heal them."

This passage is talking about both natural eyes and spiritual eyes. Jesus was constantly trying to get people to understand there is more than just the natural.

Luke 8:46; "And Jesus said, Somebody hath touched me: for I perceive that virtue is gone out of me."

This next verse comes from the time when Paul was going to Rome. When they were getting ready to put Paul on the boat, he spoke the following.

Acts 27:10; "And said unto them, Sirs, I perceive that this voyage will be with hurt and much damage, not only of the lading and ship, but also of our lives."

He was not seeing something in the natural because they hadn't gotten on the boat yet. There wasn't any sign of a storm. It didn't look like the weather was bad and yet Paul said he perceived.

Every place we see the word perceive it is the word *eido*. It means to see something, to pick up something, to understand something in the spirit, to get some information from another dimension.

~Living in the Realm of Revelation~

There are two dimensions. One is a natural dimension and the other a supernatural, invisible dimension. There is a natural dimension we can see and an invisible dimension that we cannot see. I want to tell you plainly that everything you see in the natural came from that other dimension which is supernatural and invisible. Because it did, we need to understand how powerful this other dimension is and begin to perceive it, move into it and tap into it. Begin to operate in the revelatory secrets of looking into another dimension and begin to operate according to a higher dimension.

What is in the spirit supersedes what is in the natural. Everything in the natural was created from that which is in the supernatural. Therefore, if you want to make any changes in the natural you have to go into the supernatural where the natural came from. Otherwise, you are putting a band-aid on an issue and never change it. If you want to deal with the fruit, you have to get to the root and the root is in the dimension of the supernatural. God's people have to quit operating by the flesh. We have to quit operating like carnal, natural, mortal beings because we are more than that.

We are supernatural spiritual beings and the Spirit of God dwells on the inside of us. There is a part of us that is eternal, a part of us that is supernatural, a part of us that will live forever and ever and that is the part we need to focus on the most. I didn't say to totally ignore the natural. We deal with it. Anything that needs to be naturally done, you do it. But don't ignore the supernatural, invisible realm because that is how you bring permanent change into the natural.

Acts 14:8-10; "And there sat a certain man at Lystra, impotent in his feet, being a cripple from his mother's womb, who never had walked: The same heard Paul speak: who stedfastly beholding him, and perceiving that he had faith to be healed, Said with a loud voice, Stand upright on thy feet. And he leaped and walked."

Let's take note of what happed. The man of God preached a message, looked at the man who was crippled and perceived that this man had faith to be healed.

~Living in the Realm of Revelation~

There are times when I minister to people that I know are not going to get healed. I perceive it. They are expecting me to do it and are not using any faith of their own. They will look at me because I have a healing ministry, which I do. But it takes that persons faith connecting with mine to produce the miracle they need.

Matthew 18:19; "Again I say unto you, That if two of you shall agree on earth as touching any thing that they shall ask, it shall be done for them of my Father which is in heaven."

All through the Word of God Jesus would make statements like this: Do you believe I am able to do this? If you can believe all things are possible to him who believes.

Two blind men came to Jesus. He asked what they wanted and did they believe He could do it. Think about it. Jesus is the healer and He is requiring these blind people to believe.

I don't always lay hands on everyone who is sick. Jesus didn't. He went to the pool of Bethesda and only healed one person. You would think He would have cleared the hospital out. Read John 5 about the pool of Bethesda yourself.

Thousands of sick people were at the hospital we know as the Pool of Bethesda. There were five different levels that we can call wards or divisions. Jesus went to one person. Why to only one? In the spirit he was that one person who would believe it, receive it and it was the time for that one person to come up into a place of healing.

I heard one minister say we need to learn to pick the fruit that is ripe instead of the fruit that is green. When you come into the house of God, not everybody's fruit is ripe. That means not everybody's faith is ready to receive a miracle. They might get ready before the service ends and somebody can get into the spirit, perceive who has it and who doesn't. There is no way to find out in the natural. Someone can be saying amen and still not have it. They can be shouting and dancing and still not have it. You can't look at the natural to determine what is supernatural. There is no way to know it.

"Well if someone dances and shouts a lot it means they are spiritual." No, it doesn't. I have seen people who didn't dance or shout and yet were very spiritual, powerful and plugged into the realm of the spirit. That doesn't mean we shouldn't dance, shout and do all of that. It does mean we can't just look at someone and make a determination.

I have been in meetings when witches came in. They were dancing and praising. The average person in a church would think they were spiritual. No, they were not because they had the wrong spirit. The moment you take authority, it shuts them down. Start moving in the glory and it shuts them down.

We must quit looking at the natural to determine the supernatural. Everybody who calls themselves a Christian isn't. Some have hidden agendas and we need to discern that. Not everyone is of God. We have to perceive in the spirit realm and pick up the right information about the way things really are.

Illumination

God wants to illuminate us. Light is always synonymous with revelation and illumination.

1 John 1:7; "But if we walk in the light [of revelation]**, as he is in the light, we have fellowship one with another, and the blood of Jesus Christ his Son cleanseth us from all sin."**

Fellowship with one another is koinonia. God is going to talk to us and we can talk to Him. We can ask questions and He will answer them if we are walking in the light. We need to be in that light of revelation because that is where He is. Where He is is where we are going to have fellowship with one another. Fellowship one with another means we can ask Him questions and He will answer, train us, equip us and teach us to move in the realm of the spirit.

~Living in the Realm of Revelation~

Be Aware of Things in the Spirit

There have been times in my life when I have been going through the motions, not aware of anything. I am half-asleep spiritually. Can you admit it also? Haven't we all been there? I don't want to stay there. I want to be awakened.

In Joel 3:9 we read, *"Wake up the mighty men."* What does that mean? They weren't asleep naturally, but they were spiritually. I don't want to be a person who is just coasting spiritually; unaware of anything that is going on in the spirit.

In Genesis 28 there is a very unique story about Jacob. I have preached from it many times and still get awesome revelation. We know about Jacob's ladder, what happened when the heavens opened and calling that place Bethel. I encourage you to read this story.

Genesis 28:16; "And Jacob awaked out of his sleep, and he said, Surely the LORD is in this place; and I knew it not."

He wasn't aware until the Lord started manifesting, although evidently He had been there all along.

God doesn't have to manifest for Him to be in a place. Just because He is not manifesting doesn't mean He isn't there. The Lord is a very present help in time of need. He said in Hebrew 13:15 and in Mathew 28:20 "He would never leave us or forsake us and would be with us always even to the end of the world." So, whether you know it or not He is with you. He is in you, for you and He wants us to be aware of it.

I think there are times when we need to sit down in our prayer time, put our hand on our belly and say, *"Lord, you are in me. Lord, you are with me. I am aware of you, not by feelings but by faith, the Word of God and my spiritual perception."*

What would happen if you and I were more perceptive and aware of Him? He would manifest Himself more to us, in us and through us.

When the Spirit of God begins moving just the least little bit in a service, we need to acknowledge Him. The moment you do, His power will get stronger for you.

When someone knocks on your door and you acknowledge them, they come into the room and you do more talking. What if someone knocks on your door and you can see but do not acknowledge them? They are not going to come in, sup with you and you with them.

Revelation 3:20; "Behold, I stand at the door, and knock: if any man hear my voice, and open the door, I will come in to him, and will sup with him, and he with me."

That scripture was not written to the sinner but to the saint. Jesus is in your life, but He is standing at the door knocking, waiting for you to invite Him in so you two can communicate. He wants to talk to you more. He can only do that if you are aware He is there wanting to talk, teach, and impart.

We need to ask to be more aware of His indwelling presence, of His glory, of who He is in and with us. He is Emmanuel. If you have accepted Jesus as your Lord and Savior, He is resident in you. He is also resident with you as Emmanuel. He is for you also. If God be for you, who can be against you.

So, He is for you, with you and in you. The more you acknowledge and make yourself aware of that the more He is going to manifest, talk to you, commune with you, minister to you and teach you all things.

The moment that you make yourself aware let me tell you what else will happen. You will be going along and realize there is a heightened angelic presence with you. Acknowledge and thank the Lord that you are aware He has sent more angels to be around you. Also ask Him to let you know if you need to know anything else. There is usually a reason for that.

Being Sensitive

We need to sensitize ourselves to the atmosphere around us.

In Luke 5:15-17, Jesus was teaching the Word and the presence of the Lord was present to heal them. What does that mean? The atmosphere became charged with a healing anointing. Even though Jesus is the healer, there was a greater atmosphere of healing that came.

Four men who were carrying their sick friend recognized it. They became aware that the power of healing had come into that building. The decision was made that whatever they had to do to get their friend into that atmosphere, they were going to do it. They recognized and became sensitized to a move of the Spirit of God in that building. Was everybody aware of it? I don't believe so. You can only benefit from what you are aware of.

We must become very sensitive.

Several years ago I heard Lester Sumrall tell a story. He had been mentoring Rod Parsley and they were speaking at a series of meetings on healing. Oral Roberts had been invited to come, but had said he couldn't make it. They were sitting on the platform getting ready to begin the service. All of a sudden Lester Sumrall put his hand on his belly, told Rod Parsley to do the same and asked if he sensed something. Rod replied that he did and the healing anointing had just increased in the building. Lester told him Oral Roberts was somewhere in the building. In a short time, Oral Roberts came and sat down next to Rod Parsley. His schedule had changed and not having time to tell anyone, he decided to just show up. This is what I mean by sensitizing ourselves.

You should be able to tell when the prophet has walked into the room before you see him. You should be able to tell when an apostle moves in because you feel another level of authority even without your natural eyes seeing him.

God wants to bring us to a greater sensitivity, but it won't happen if we don't practice it. We must make ourselves aware of it and yield to it.

Mark 3:1-5; "And he entered again into the synagogue; and there was a man there which had a withered hand. And they watched him, whether he would heal him on the sabbath day; that they might accuse him. And he saith unto the man which had the withered hand, Stand forth. And he saith unto them, Is it lawful to do good on the sabbath days, or to do evil? to save life, or to kill? But they held their peace. And when he had looked round about on them with anger, being grieved for the hardness of their hearts, he saith unto the man, Stretch forth thine hand. And he stretched it out: and his hand was restored whole as the other."

There is a thing that makes us hard hearted when we don't care about the needs of others. When we care more about being religiously or politically correct, we are no longer sensitive to people.

The Pharisees and Sadducees had so many rules and regulations that they no longer cared about the needs of people. They only cared about being religiously correct. Jesus didn't come to be religiously correct. He came to seek and save that which was lost. Jesus came to heal the sick, to cleanse the leper, to raise the dead, to cast out devils, to preach the Word of God to the people, to bring changes in the hearts of people, and bring salvation to the lost. His main thing was that He must minister to the people.

Religion is rules and regulations and how you go about it. *"You can only heal them on a certain day in a certain way or it is not of God."* Everything has to be done the way they tell you how to do it according to their law and their interpretation of it. You have to wear the right kind of clothes and have a certain pious look. You have to do it in the right way and use all the right words. We have religious ideas that we follow. We must have church on Sunday morning and that is the only time. I know people who are that way. They have their routine down and are not going to change it. It makes no difference what God wants to do.

When we do that we are not sensitive to other people. When we lose the sensitivity to the needs of people and put rules, regulations and our religious ideas above ministering to people then we become hard hearted. If you are not sensitive to the needs of people, you will not be sensitive to God. If you can't hurt because somebody else is hurting, you will not feel the presence of God, or know the heart of God.

I want to tell you something about Jesus. He wasn't religious. He didn't always wear the right clothes and do the right thing according to religious standards. Constantly criticized, He was told He had a devil was accused of doing things for the money and having the wrong attitude as well as wanting to mess up their ways. All He wanted to do was reveal the will of the Father to man and minister to people.

Hebrews 4:15; "For we have not an high priest which cannot be touched with the feeling of our infirmities; but was in all points tempted like as we are, yet without sin."

We have to get to the place where we feel for people in our spirit man. Oral Roberts would cry with just the thought of somebody suffering with sickness. That is what it takes to have a healing ministry. You have to hate sickness with all your heart and cry with the people who are hurting or sick. If you will then gifts of healings will kick in. You will be around somebody and start feeling their pain. It is not that you are feeling it in your flesh, but in your spirit man. Your spirit man has five senses just like your natural man does.[8]

There are times when I get around someone that I can tell when they are hurting emotionally. I can feel the difference. I am sensitive enough that I can tell when they are angry, have had losses or have joy. I can also tell when something great or something bad has happened.

I sense it and am sensitive to it because I have made myself sensitive to it. I care. When you care about others, your spiritual sense of feeling reaches out and connects with them. You want to alleviate their suffering and pain.

The selfish attitude of only caring about ourselves is what shuts down sensitivity. Selfishness will make you hard hearted. Do whatever it takes to get rid of selfishness in your life. My life is not about me but

---

[8] The third course of our School of the Prophets teaches on the five spiritual senses, how they operate, how you can activate them and get them operative in your life. For more information visit our website: www.prophetphilrich.com.

about others. Everything is going to be all right for me as long as I put somebody else first. Seek first the kingdom of God and His righteousness and all these things will be added.

There are times when we need to pray and reach out with our spiritual emotional feelings toward other people. Just take time to think about somebody else and how they must feel, what they must be going through and you will begin becoming very sensitive to the Holy Spirit and the needs of other people.

Correct Focus

We have to focus on the right thing.

2 Corinthians 4:18; "While we look not at the things which are seen, but at the things which are not seen: for the things which are seen are temporal; but the things which are not seen are eternal."

Paul is telling us not to consider what we see in the natural to be of any great value because it can change at any moment.

Look at the things that are not seen. Consider that which isn't seen.

I learned a long time ago not only to just listen to what my children say, but to also listen to what they don't say. Listen for something that is left out. My mom always knew what I was doing even if I didn't tell her.

In other words, Paul is telling us to focus. What are you focusing on? Did you know that your focus determines the direction of your life? That is why they put blinders on the sides of the head of racehorses. The blinders keep them focused straight ahead. If the horse is focused on something to the side, that is the direction they will go. We do the same thing when we are driving. Ever look off to the side and find you are driving that direction? In other words, the direction of your life is based on focus.

If you are focusing on the things of the spirit, guess what will happen. You will experience the things of the spirit and will go into the spirit realm.

Monitoring the Realm of the Spirit

Proverbs 20:27; "The spirit of man is the candle of the LORD, searching all the inward parts of the belly."

Your inner man is in the inner region of you. That is where the Holy Spirit dwells. He dwells in your spirit.

Your spirit is the candle that God is going to use to illuminate, speak and reveal to you. He will not use your natural head, but your inner man.

Someone will come up to me to say something. On the inside I will monitor what is happening and what they are saying based on what the Holy Spirit in me is letting me know about them and what they are saying. I have had people tell me things and I knew on the inside it was not one hundred percent correct.

One lady needed counseling. While she was talking I heard this on the inside, *"She wants to talk. She doesn't want the solution. She wants somebody to listen to her."* I told her that I would give her only four sessions. At the first one I would listen to her troubles. For the next three sessions I would not listen to her troubles, but would help her come out of her situation. She said that I didn't understand, that she had been through a lot of things. I answered I knew and was giving her the first session to say it all. At our next session she started in with her problems. I stopped her saying I didn't want to hear about them and that we were going to work with helping her. She didn't like that. The Holy Spirit had already told me she wasn't there for help. She wanted to talk.

Nine out of ten times the people don't want a solution because a solution means they cannot be there to bend your ear. They would have to get rid of the problem and receive the restoration and healing they needed. Rarely will people ever tell you the real problem. They will skirt it every time. Seldom will they admit they messed up. It is always somebody else's fault.

I told one woman there was more than one person she had unforgiveness toward. One was her mother, the other her stepmother. She began crying saying she couldn't deal with what her stepmother had done. I said we needed to cancel the counseling session then since she wasn't going to deal with the unforgiveness. I couldn't help her.

See what happens when you monitor the realm of the spirit?

Other times I will know why somebody is not getting their healing or I will know what is really wrong with them. You can look at somebody with a broken arm and say we need to pray for the broken arm. The Holy Spirit may tell you that their equilibrium is off and that is why they are falling. Pray for the equilibrium.

I may look at someone and it will look like there isn't anything wrong with them. In my spirit though I know something was wrong. Maybe something happened to them as a little child. When they ask how I knew that all I can say is that I knew it inside my spirit. I might go on to say they were around seven years old when someone hurt them badly. They will begin weeping. I told another person I saw them him when he was a little boy crawl into a closet to hide and cry while his mom and dad fought. He wept through the night. This is getting to the root through the revelatory realm.

We all can do it. What you proclaim you produce. I am proclaiming it so you can do it. I am teaching it so it will happen in your life.

Go Past the Veil of the Flesh

Go past the veil of the flesh if you want to move in the spirit.

I want to show you something about dealing with the flesh and then being led by the spirit. If you don't deal with the flesh you will never be led by the spirit. You can't be led by both the flesh and the spirit at the same time because they contradict each other.

~Living in the Realm of Revelation~

Romans 8:13-14; "For if ye live after the flesh, ye shall die: but if ye through the Spirit do mortify the deeds of the body, ye shall live. For as many as are led by the Spirit of God, they are the sons of God."

"Live after" means your focus in on you, your appetites, your desire, your wishes, your wants. It is me, me, me, me.

Through the spirit you mortify the deeds of the body. You can't control your flesh by yourself. You will fail.

"Well, I am just going to restrict myself and tell myself no." You will be telling yourself no while you are doing it. You need the power of the Holy Spirit.

Mortify comes from the word mortician. The mortar that you use to keep bricks together comes from the same word also.

You have to stop the deeds of the body through the power of the Holy Spirit. Kill the flesh. Tell your flesh it is not going to do what it wants to do. By the power of the Spirit command it to come in line and with the power of the Spirit you enforce it. In other words, you are going to pray when your flesh doesn't want to.

Call a prayer meeting and see how many people show up. One pastor did that and had about five out of his 300 people congregation show up. He had a ham and bean supper and 300 people showed up. The following week he called for a prayer meeting and had five show up. This pastor resigned and told the people they cared more about beans than God.

I believe people care about God, but there is a battle. The more I pray, the more power I have in God and the more I can operate in the realm of the spirit. Then why don't I pray more? It is because I am battling me. I am battling satan and my flesh who don't want me to. In order for me to have bible study, read the word and pray every day, I am going to have to mortify the deeds of my body through the Spirit. Notice, you can't do it by yourself. If you are failing, don't beat yourself. You just have to do it by the power of the Spirit and ask God for special grace.

~Living in the Realm of Revelation~

When I am battling to pray, I pray about it. It works for me every time. I am honest with God and I tell Him I am sorry, that I am battling prayerlessness. I need to pray and want to. I ask for the power and grace to do it. I ask him to help me set myself in order by the power of the Spirit. In just a day or two I am back into the routine of praying every day like I am supposed to. I have learned to set up a time and a place to pray. My reason to pray is to be near God. If you don't have a time, place and purpose you won't pray. The devil will steal your prayer life from you. Set a time to pray and make sure it is a good time, a time when you can do it. Have a place to pray and a purpose to pray. The purpose should be to be intimate with God. If you pray just to get needs met, you will miss it.

You take authority over your flesh, make it obey you and then you move on into the Holy of Holies face to face with God.

Luke 16:16; "The law and the prophets were until John: since that time the kingdom of God is preached, and every man presseth into it."

You have to press into the kingdom and push into it. You push through the veil of your own flesh and rend your flesh. Once you get past the flesh, you can move into the spirit. Once you defeat your own flesh there isn't anything you can't do in the spirit realm.

Hearing God

We are going to talk about hearing God in a way that does come against the flesh, hearing God even when it comes to sacrifices and offerings. You will never be spiritually what you should be until you can hear God in your offerings and giving.

In my life, I learned to move deeper in words of knowledge when I started listening to God in what I was supposed to give. There have been times when my wife and I would confer on things. When I was right on regarding what I was supposed to be doing it would start to build a confidence in me that I had heard the voice of God. Before long the same voice that told me how much to give in an offering was telling me somebody's name, somebody's illness. It was not a different voice, but the same one. You can develop your spirit through hearing God in giving. A lot of people don't like to hear this, but this is one way you can radically build your spirit man high.

Genesis 22:1-2; "And it came to pass after these things, that God did tempt Abraham, and said unto him, Abraham: and he said, Behold, here I am. And he said, Take now thy son, thine only son Isaac, whom thou lovest, and get thee into the land of Moriah; and offer him there for a burnt offering upon one of the mountains which I will tell thee of."

God didn't come to him and say He would like Abraham to give an offering and anything he wanted to give was okay so long as he gave something. It wouldn't matter what it was.

Genesis 22:16-18; "And said, By myself have I sworn, saith the LORD, for because thou hast done this thing, and hast not withheld thy son, thine only son: That in blessing I will bless thee, and in multiplying I will multiply thy seed as the stars of the heaven, and as the sand which is upon the sea shore; and thy seed shall possess the gate of his enemies; And in thy seed shall all the nations of the earth be blessed; because thou hast obeyed my voice."

Abraham didn't get his blessings by just giving anything. He got his blessing by listening to and obeying the voice of God.

There is an offering God wants you to give, a sacrifice He requires.

There were four compromises Pharaoh tried to give Moses prior to him leading the people out of Egypt. Are you aware of them?

When Moses asked Pharaoh to let the people go so that they could give sacrifice to God, Pharaoh said they could give sacrifice there. Moses answered that they couldn't give sacrifice while they were in bondage.

Then Pharaoh told him not to go very far, just go three days journey. Now satan is telling us not to pray all the time, not to go to church all the time, and not be radical. Just get saved and live your life. Demonic pharaohs are still saying the same thing to the church today. Moses said they were not going three days, but going all the way.

When that didn't work, Pharaoh called Moses back and said all the men could go. The women, children and all their belongings had to stay behind. Again, Moses said no, whole families were going to go. The devil will tell you that it is okay for you to be saved, just don't expect your mate or family to get saved also. You need to say, "*No, devil. We are all coming out.*"

The fourth compromise Pharaoh offered was this. "Go and take all the families, but leave all the possessions behind". Moses answered with something interesting. No, they were taking all the cattle, finances, gold, silver because once they got out there they had no idea what God would require them to sacrifice to Him.

Moses didn't say it was their money and they might want to build something with it. Many Christians would give that reason for keeping their finances and goods. They want a house at the lake, a condo in town and cars in both locations.

I am not against having nice houses or cars. Just how many houses can you live in? How many cars can you drive before it is just flesh, worshipping self and not pleasing God? Become balanced in these areas.

Philippians 4:18-19; "But I have all, and abound: I am full, having received of Epaphroditus the things which were sent from you, an odour of a sweet smell, a sacrifice acceptable, wellpleasing to God. But my God shall supply all your need according to his riches in glory by Christ Jesus."

We all want to read Philippians 4:19. We want to shout over verse 19 and skip verse 18, but you don't get 19 until you have done 18.

If Paul is saying there is an offering that is acceptable, a sacrifice that is acceptable and well pleasing then there must be a sacrifice that is not well pleasing or acceptable. Which one is acceptable and well pleasing? It is the one the Lord requires of you, the one the Lord speaks to you to do.

~Living in the Realm of Revelation~

When your offering is acceptable, well pleasing and has a sweet smell then the Lord sends fire and glory. He consumes the burnt sacrifice and pours His glory all over you. If He doesn't like your offering, He doesn't accept it. You lose it because it is still gone but you get nothing from it. Attitude has something to do with whether or not it smells good.

"God should just accept anything I want to give." That sounds like a Cain and Abel situation. Cain gave his best vegetables even though God wanted an animal sacrifice. It is not giving God what you want but what He wants that is received.

Chapter 5
Impartation Increases Revelation

If you are around somebody who is full of the revelation of God's Word and who moves by revelation gifts and revelation power and connect with them, then what is in and on them will come into and be on you.

Romans 1:11-12; "For I long to see you, that I may impart unto you some spiritual gift, to the end ye may be established; That is, that I may be comforted together with you by the mutual faith both of you and me."

They didn't have television, videos or skype back then. If you wanted to see someone, you had to go to where they were. You had to visit them.

Paul not only said he had something to impart to them, they also had something to impart to him. In other words, every born again, Spirit filled child of God has something to impart.

When I ministered in Germany I found out that in German there is no translation for the word impartation. The closest word the translators could use was implantation – to implant, to put something in you from somebody else.

When I looked at the word impart in the Greek I found it has two parts to it. The first part is *meta* (*met-ah'*). *Meta* means participation, proximity and sequence. In other words, in order to have an impartation you have to be participating with somebody else. You have to be connecting and helping somebody do something. The next part of the definition was proximity. How close are you to them? I am not talking about being physically close but heart to heart. How connected are you to their heart? Sequence – how often do you connect with them? How often do you read their material, hear them preach or are around them.

The second part of the word impartation is *didomi* (*did'-o-mee*). This word means to bestow, bring forth, grant or to commit. While you are connecting heart to heart to a ministry, participating with a ministry what happens is that there is a bestowing of the anointing that is upon them to you. There is a granting, a committing of something to you that you didn't have before.

Paul was saying he longed to be with, to see the Romans in order for that to happen.

I want to give you four ways that this impartation can take place.

Perception

You have to first perceive that a man or woman of God has something to give you. If you look at them and say you don't think they have anything, then you won't get anything from them. You must first perceive before you can ever receive.

I want to look at a story about Elijah and Elisha and how the mantle was passed to Elisha.

2 Kings 2:9-10; "And it came to pass, when they were gone over, that Elijah said unto Elisha, Ask what I shall do for thee, before I be taken away from thee. And Elisha said, I pray thee, let a double portion of thy spirit be upon me. And he said, Thou hast asked a hard thing: nevertheless, <u>if thou see me</u> when I am taken from thee, it shall be so unto thee; but if not, it shall not be so."

<u>"See"</u> in this verse means to perceive or to discern.

Elisha had to perceive who Elijah was and what he had or he wouldn't get anything.

2 Kings 2:11-12; "And it came to pass, as they still went on, and talked, that, behold, there appeared a chariot of fire, and horses of fire, and parted them both asunder; and Elijah went up by a whirlwind into heaven. And Elisha saw it, and he cried, My father, my father, the chariot of Israel, and the horsemen thereof. And he saw him no more: and he took hold of his own clothes, and rent them in two pieces."

Elisha saw it and cried out, "my father, my father". What was he seeing? It was the very thing the prophet said he would have to see.

What was it he perceived? He cried out my father, my father. He wasn't crying out to the Heavenly Father. Father in the Hebrew is *ab* (*awb*). It has to do with patrimony or a father who has an inheritance to be given to a son.

Elisha saw who the prophet really was to him. The prophet was a spiritual father who had an impartation, something to give to someone who became a spiritual son. Elisha was able to take hold of that mantle and receive it because he could perceive who the man of God was and what the man of God had for him.

You can never receive what you cannot first perceive. The level of your perception is the level of your reception.

As God connects you with fivefold ministry and you start receiving the gifts within them, don't look at the flesh. Don't stop with how good they can teach or preach. It is much more than that. What is deep on the inside of them? What about the gifts of God, the mantles, the anointing, and the glory they carry? What about the authority and the Spirit of God that moves in and through them? What about the level of revelation they are operating in both in the Word and in the spirit? Can you discern all of that?

Instead of getting jealous, realize if you connect to it and perceive it then you can receive it. Quit looking at somebody and say you wish you were anointed like that. Stop wishing and start believing, connecting, perceiving and receiving.

Connection

In order to come into the full place of impartation there has to be connection along with perception.

Numbers 11:24-25; "And Moses went out, and told the people the words of the LORD, and gathered the seventy men of the elders of the people, and set them round about the tabernacle. And the LORD came down in a cloud, and spake unto him, and took of the spirit that was upon him, and gave it unto the seventy elders: and it came to pass, that, when the spirit rested upon them, they prophesied, and did not cease."

Moses' father Jethro had come to him saying that he was trying to judge and minister to three and a half million people. Moses would kill himself because he was overdoing it. Jethro told him to raise up seventy men that were faithful who would help and assist him. These were the seventy referred to in verse 24.

The seventy elders had connected with the man of God to help, aid and assist. They received the spirit that was on Moses.

We need to know these things so that we will not be lacking in any mantle or anointing. Instead of just a few super anointed men and women of God, there will be super anointed churches filled with people who move in the fire, power and glory of God.

Association

Proverbs 13:20; "He that walketh with wise men shall be wise: but a companion of fools shall be destroyed."

If you hang out with fools, you become a fool like them.

As humans, we are very impressionable people. When I was in Bible school they had me take a psychology course. I learned that it was believed that 90-95% of our personality comes from those we associated with. Now they are saying it is 95-97%. Only 3% has to do with the family you were born into. Heredity really does not develop your personality.

Scripture has more to say about who we hang out with. Look at what it says about associating with an angry man.

Proverbs 22:24-25; "Make no friendship with an angry man; and with a furious man thou shalt not go: Lest thou learn his ways, and get a snare to thy soul."

There is a saying that goes birds of a feather flock together. You become like the company you keep. You are responsible for developing your own personality based upon who you connect to. Who do you listen to and hang out with? What ministries are you connected to? You will be just like them, having all their gifts.

2 Timothy 1:5; "When I call to remembrance the unfeigned faith that is in thee, <u>which dwelt first</u> in thy grandmother Lois, and thy mother Eunice; and I am persuaded that in thee also."

Unfeigned faith is faith that is real and not hypocritical.

Paul is saying that your associations will determine what you will be like and what you will have in your life.

Are you understanding these laws of impartation to move in revelation?

Communication

Philippians 4:15; "Now ye Philippians know also, that in the beginning of the gospel, when I departed from Macedonia, no church communicated with me as concerning giving and receiving, but ye only."

The word communicate actually means koinonia – to fellowship with, to connect to.

When you support a ministry you are communicating something to them. First, you are saying to that ministry you see God in them. You are also saying they are worthy to be supported. Then you are also saying you are thankful God blessed you through that ministry so you want to bless the ministry by making sure they have the money to travel to another location. The last thing you are saying to that ministry is that you want to stand with them so that together you can spread the gospel.

Pastors know well that tithes and offerings communicate. I have heard pastors say that when the people are tithing and giving they are voting on the success of the church and are backing the pastor. When they stop tithing and giving they are also communicating something and it is not positive. Pastors can tell when someone is going to leave the church based on their giving record. They start backing off on their offering and tithe.

I want to show you that communication is another step to receiving impartation from a ministry.

Philippians 1:3-5; "I thank my God upon every remembrance of you, Always in every prayer of mine for you all making request with joy, For your fellowship [koinonia, communication] **in the gospel from the first day until now;"**

Paul was referring to their regular offerings from the first day until the present.

Philippians 1:6; "Being confident of this very thing, that he which hath begun a good work in you will perform it until the day of Jesus Christ:"

Because they had been faithfully supporting his ministry God would faithfully bless them.

Philippians 1:7; "Even as it is meet [right] **for me to think this of you all, because I have you in my heart** [partnership]**; inasmuch as both in my bonds, and in the defence and confirmation of the gospel, ye all are partakers of my grace."**

Confirmation of the gospel means all nine manifestations of the Spirit.

Paul said that because they were a partner they were a partaker of what he had. What you partner with, you get a part of. What you sow into, you tap into spiritually and financially. God's Word works when you work God's Word.

1 Kings 19:15-18; "And the LORD said unto him [Elijah]**, Go, return on thy way to the wilderness of Damascus: and when thou comest, anoint Hazael to be king over Syria: And Jehu the son of Nimshi shalt thou anoint to be king over Israel: and Elisha the son of Shaphat of Abelmeholah shalt thou anoint to be prophet in thy room. And it shall come to pass, that him that escapeth the sword of Hazael shall Jehu slay: and him that escapeth from the sword of Jehu shall Elisha slay. Yet I have left me seven thousand in Israel, all the knees which have not bowed unto Baal, and every mouth which hath not kissed him."**

The Lord was answering a question about the time when Elijah was having a pity party thinking he was the only one who really served the Lord. There were seven thousand others.

1 Kings 19:19; "So he departed thence, and found Elisha the son of Shaphat, who was plowing with twelve yoke of oxen before him, and he with the twelfth: and Elijah passed by him, and cast his mantle upon him."

Casting his mantle upon him means Elijah released an anointing on Elisha. He didn't leave the mantle with Elisha, but just let him feel it.

1 Kings 19:20; "And he left the oxen, and ran after Elijah, and said, Let me, I pray thee, kiss my father and my mother, and then I will follow thee. And he said unto him, Go back again: for what have I done to thee?"

Elijah was telling him that if he wanted the anointing to come get it. If not, then he would go on to the next person. When you find an Elijah, he doesn't chase you. You chase after the Elijah. You are not following after a man but a mantle. When people say you are following a man, tell them you are following after a mantle that God has released upon a man of God. Paul said to follow him as he followed Christ. If Paul said that, then evidently there are some men and women of God you are supposed to follow.

1 Kings 19:21 And he [Elisha] returned back from him, and took a yoke of oxen, and slew them, and boiled their flesh with the instruments of the oxen, and gave unto the people, and they did eat. Then he arose, and went after Elijah, and ministered unto him.

Elisha went after Elijah.

Who is the one who is supposed to do the connecting? Elisha or Elijah? If you are going to be an Elisha, it is your responsibility to connect heart to heart. You have to say you are going to support a ministry, pray for that ministry, get their materials and listen to their teachings. You will attend their meetings when they are in your area.

Minister in the Hebrew is *sharath* (*shaw-rath'*). It means to attend to, to wait on and to contribute unto. It ties in with some verses in Luke.

Luke 8:1-3; "And it came to pass afterward, that he went throughout every city and village, preaching and shewing the glad tidings of the kingdom of God: and the twelve were with him, And certain women, which had been healed of evil spirits and infirmities, Mary called Magdalene, out of whom went seven devils, And Joanna the wife of

Chuza Herod's steward, and Susanna, and many others, which ministered unto him of their substance."

How do you minister to the man of God? It is not going to them and giving them a prophecy, though that may happen at times. They need someone to pray for them and financially support them. They must have both.

So, learn to serve the Elijah's God has given you. Listen to and observe how they move and operate in the Spirit. Then chase after that mantle and attain it. The mantles you receive from the Elijah's that you connect to will determine the success you will have in fulfilling your destiny.

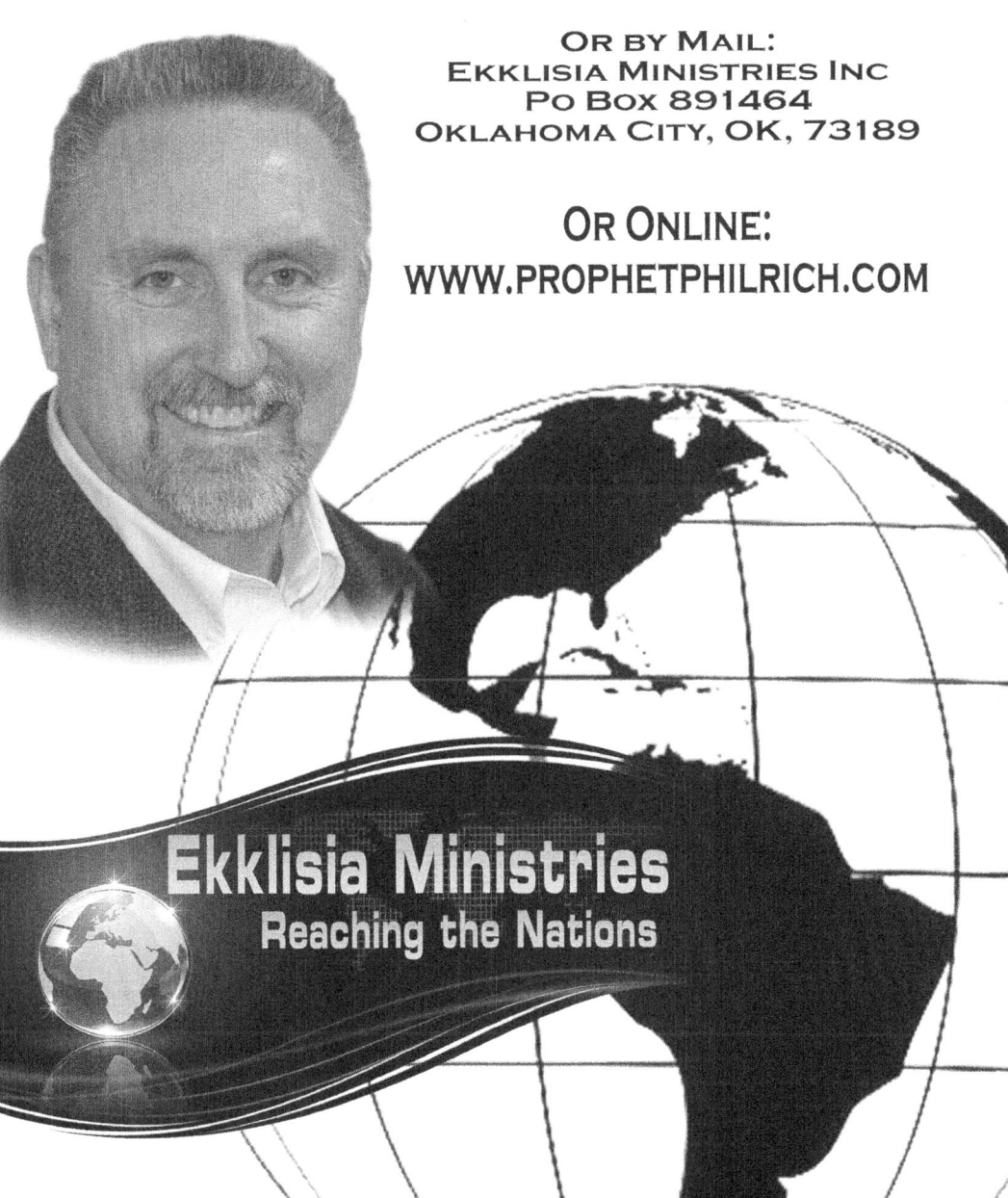

Made in the USA
Monee, IL
20 April 2021